Christ Altogether Lovely
John Flavel

Christ Altogether Lovely

By

John Flavel

Christ Altogether Lovely
John Flavel

Christ Altogether Lovely
John Flavel

Published By Parables
April, 2020

All Rights Reserved. No part of this book may be reproduced or utilized in any form or by any means, electronic or mechanical, including photocopying, recording, or by any information storage and retrieval system, without permission in writing from the author.

    ISBN 978-1-951497-65-1
    Printed in the United States of America

Readers should be aware that Internet Web sites offered as citations and/or sources for further information may have been changed or disappeared between the time this was written and the time it is read.

CHRIST ALTOGETHER LOVELY

By

John Flavel

PUBLISHED by PARABLES
Earthly Stories with a Heavenly Meaning

Christ Altogether Lovely
John Flavel

Christh Altogether Lovely
John Flavel

CONTENTS

- Christ is to be Loved
- What is Meant by "Altogether Lovely"
- He is Lovely in His Person
- He is Lovely in His Offices
- He is Lovely in His Relations
- Application

Christ Altogether Lovely
John Flavel

Christ Altogether Lovely
John Flavel

Christ is to be Loved

"Yes, He is altogether lovely." Song of Songs 5:16.

At the ninth verse of this chapter, you have a question put forth by the daughters of Jerusalem, "What is your beloved more than another beloved?" The spouse answers, "He is the chief among ten thousand." She then recounts many of the things she finds so excellent in her beloved and then concludes with these words that I have read: "Yes, he is altogether lovely."

The words set forth the transcendent loveliness of the Lord Jesus Christ, and naturally resolve themselves into three parts:

1. Who he is.
2. What he is.
3. What he is like.

First, *Who he is*: the Lord Jesus Christ, after whom she had been seeking, for whom she was overcome by love; concerning whom these daughters of Jerusalem had enquired: whom she had struggled to describe in his particular excellencies. He is the great and excellent subject of whom she here speaks.

Secondly, *What he is*, or what she claims of him: That he is a lovely one. The Hebrew word, which is often translated "desires," means "to earnestly desire, covet, or long after that which is most pleasant, graceful, delectable and admirable." The original word is both in the abstract, and plural in number, which says that Christ is the very essence of all delights and pleasures, the very soul and substance of them. As all the rivers are gathered into the ocean, which is the meeting-place of all the waters in the world, so Christ is that ocean in which all true delights and pleasures meet.

Thirdly, *What he is like*: He is altogether lovely, the every part to be desired. He is lovely when taken together, and in every part; as if she had said, "Look on him in what respect or particular you wish; cast your eye upon this lovely object, and view him any way, turn him in your serious thoughts which way you wish; consider his person, his offices, his works, or any other thing belonging to him; you will find him altogether lovely, There is nothing disagreeable in him, there is nothing lovely without him." Hence note,

DOCTRINE: That Jesus Christ is the loveliest person souls can set their eyes upon: "Thou art fairer than the children of men." Psalm 45:2.

Christ Altogether Lovely
John Flavel

He is "Altogether Lovely"

Here it is said of Jesus Christ, which cannot be said of any mere creature, that he is "altogether lovely." In opening this point I shall,

1. Examine the importance of this phrase "altogether lovely."
2. Show you in what respect Christ is so.

What is Meant by "Altogether Lovely"

Let us consider this excellent expression, and particularly reflect on what is contained in it, and you shall find this expression "altogether lovely."

First, *It excludes all unloveliness and disagreeableness from Jesus Christ*. As a theologian long ago said, "There is nothing in him which is not loveable." The excellencies of Jesus Christ are perfectly exclusive of all their opposites; there is nothing of a contrary property or quality found in him to contaminate or devaluate his excellency. And in this respect Christ infinitely transcends the most excellent and loveliest of created things. Whatsoever loveliness is found in them, it is not without a bad aftertaste. The fairest pictures must have their shadows: The rarest and most brilliant gems must have dark backgrounds to set off their beauty; the best creature is but a bitter-sweet at best: If there is something pleasing, there is also something sour: if a person has every ability, both innate and acquired, to delight us, yet there is also some natural corruption intermixed with it to put us off. But it is not so in our altogether lovely Christ, his excellencies are pure and unmixed. He is a sea of sweetness without one drop of gall.

Christ Altogether Lovely
John Flavel

Secondly, "Altogether lovely," i.e. *There is nothing unlovely found in him*, so all that is in him is wholly lovely. As every ray of God is precious, so every thing that is in Christ is precious: Who can weigh Christ in a pair of balances, and tell you what his worth is? "His price is above rubies, and all that thou canst desire is not to be compared with him," Prov. 8:11.

Thirdly "Altogether lovely," i.e. *He embraces all things that are lovely*: he seals up the sum of all loveliness. Things that shine as single stars with a particular glory, all meet in Christ as a glorious constellation. Col. 1:19, "It pleased the Father that in him should all fullness dwell." Cast your eyes among all created beings, survey the universe: you will observe strength in one, beauty in a second, faithfulness in a third, wisdom in a fourth; but you shall find none excelling in them all as Christ does. Bread has one quality, water another, raiment another, medicine another; but none has them all in itself as Christ does. He is bread to the hungry, water to the thirsty, a garment to the naked, healing to the wounded; and whatever a soul can desire is found in him, 1 Cor. 1:30.

Fourthly, "Altogether lovely," i.e. *Nothing is lovely in opposition to him, or in separation from him*. If he truly is altogether lovely, then whatsoever is opposite to him, or separate from him can have no loveliness in it. Take away Christ, and where is the loveliness of any enjoyment? The best creature-comfort apart from Christ is but a broken cistern. It cannot hold one drop of true comfort, Psalm 73:26. It is with the creature--the sweetest and loveliest creature--as with a beautiful image in the mirror: turn away the face and where is the image? Riches, honours, and comfortable relations are sweet when

Christ Altogether Lovely
John Flavel

the face of Christ smiles upon us through them; but without him, what empty trifles are they all?

Fifthly, "Altogether lovely," i.e. *Transcending all created excellencies in beauty and loveliness.* If you compare Christ and other things, no matter how lovely, no matter how excellent and desirable, Christ carries away all loveliness from them. "He is (as the apostle says) before all things," Col. 1:17. Not only before all things in time, nature, and order; but before all things in dignity, glory, and true excellence. In all things he must have the pre-eminence. Let us but compare Christ's excellence with the creature's in a few particulars, and how manifest will the transcendent loveliness of Jesus Christ appear! For,

1. All other loveliness is derived and secondary; but the loveliness of Christ is original and primary. Angels and men, the world and all the desirable things in it, receive what excellence they crave from him. They are streams from the fountain. The farther any thing departs from its fountain and original, the less excellency there is in it.

2. The loveliness and excellency of all other things, is only relative, consisting in its reference to Christ, and subservience to his glory. But Christ is lovely, considered absolutely in himself. He is desirable for himself; other things are desirable because of him.

3. The beauty and loveliness of all other things are fading and perishing; but the loveliness of Christ is fresh for all eternity. The sweetness of the best created thing is a fading flower; if not before, yet certainly at death it must fade away. Job 4:21. "Doth not their excellency, which is in them, go away?" Yes, yes, whether they are the natural excellencies of the body, acquired endowments of the mind, lovely features, graceful qualities, or anything else we find

attractive; all these like pleasant flowers are withered, faded, and destroyed by death. "But Christ is still the same, yesterday, today, and for ever," Heb. 13:8.

4. The beauty and holiness of creatures are ensnaring and dangerous. A man may make an idol out of them, and indulge himself beyond the bounds of moderation with them, but there is no danger of excess in the love of Christ. The soul is then in the healthiest frame and temper when it is most overwhelmed by love to Christ, Song of Songs 5:8.

5. The loveliness of every creature is of a confining and obstructing nature. Our esteem of it diminishes the closer we approach to it, or the longer we enjoy it. Creatures, like pictures, are fairest at a certain distance, but it is not so with Christ; the nearer the soul approaches him, and the longer it lives in the enjoyment of him, still the sweeter and more desirable he becomes.

6. All other loveliness cannot satisfy the soul of man. There is not scope enough in any one created thing, or in all the natural universe of created things for the soul of man to reach out and expand; but the soul still feels itself confined and narrowed within those limits. This comes to pass from the inadequacy and unsuitableness of the creature to the nobler and more excellent soul of man. The soul is like a ship in a narrow river which does not have room to turn. It is always running aground and foundering in the shallows. But Jesus Christ is in every way sufficient to the vast desires of the soul; in him it has sea-room enough. In him the soul may spread all its sails with no fear of touching bottom. And thus you see what is the importance of this phrase, "Altogether lovely."

Christ Altogether Lovely
John Flavel

How Christ is "Altogether Lovely"

Secondly, Next I promised to show you in what respects Jesus Christ is altogether lovely:

He is Lovely in His Person

First, He is altogether lovely in his person: he is Deity dwelling in flesh, John 1:14. The wonderful, perfect union of the divine and human nature in Christ renders him an object of admiration and adoration to both angels and men, 1 Tim. 3:16. God never presented to the world such a vision of glory before. Consider how the human nature of our Lord Jesus Christ is overflowing with all the graces of the Spirit, in such a way as never any of the saints was filled. O what a lovely picture does this paint of him! John 3:34, "God gives the Spirit [to him] without limit." This makes him "the most excellent of men and [his] lips have been anointed with grace," Psalm 45:2. If a small measure of grace in the saints makes them sweet and desirable companions, what must the riches of the Spirit of grace filling Jesus Christ without measure make him in the eyes of believers? O what a glory must it fix upon him!

Christ Altogether Lovely
John Flavel

Christ Altogether Lovely
John Flavel

He is Lovely in His Offices

Secondly, He is altogether lovely in his offices: let us consider for a moment the suitability, fullness, and comforting nature of them.

First, *The suitability of the offices of Christ to the miseries of men.* We cannot but adore the infinite wisdom of his receiving them. We are, by nature, blind and ignorant, at best but groping in the dim light of nature after God, Acts 17:27. Jesus Christ is a light to lighten the Gentiles, Isa. 49:6. When this great prophet came into the world, then did the day-spring from on high visit us, Luke 1:78. By nature we are alienated from, and at enmity against God; Christ comes into the world to be an atoning sacrifice, making peace by the blood of his cross, Col. 1:20. All the world, by nature, is in bondage and captivity to Satan, a miserable slavery. Christ comes with kingly power, to rescue sinners, as a prey from the mouth of the terrible one.

Secondly, *Let the fullness of his offices be also considered,* which make him able "to save to the uttermost, all that come to God by him," Heb. 7:25. The three offices, comprising in them all that our souls do need, become an universal relief to all our distresses; and therefore,

Thirdly, *Unspeakably comforting must the offices of Christ be to the souls of sinners.* If light be pleasant to our eyes, how pleasant is that light of life springing from the Sun of righteousness! Mal. 4:2. If a pardon be sweet to a condemned criminal, how sweet must the sprinkling the blood of Jesus be to the trembling conscience of a

Christ Altogether Lovely
John Flavel

law-condemned sinner? If a rescue from a cruel tyrant is sweet to a poor captive, how sweet must it be to the ears of enslaved sinners, to hear the voice of liberty and deliverance proclaimed by Jesus Christ? Out of the several offices of Christ, as out of so many fountains, all the promises of the new covenant flow, as so many soul-refreshing streams of peace and joy. All the promises of illumination, counsel and direction flow out of Christ's prophetic office. All the promises of reconciliation, peace, pardon, and acceptance flow out of his priestly office, with the sweet streams of joy and spiritual comforts which accompany it. All the promises of converting, increasing, defending, directing, and supplying grace, flow out of the kingly office of Christ; indeed, all promises may be reduced to these three offices, so that Jesus Christ must be altogether lovely in his offices.

Christ Altogether Lovely
John Flavel

He is Lovely in His Relations.

First, *He is a lovely Redeemer*, Isa. 61:1. He came to open the prison-doors to them that are bound. Needs must this Redeemer be a lovely one, if we consider the depth of misery from which he redeemed us, even "from the wrath to come," 1 Thess. 1:10. Consider the numbers redeemed, and the means of their redemption. Rev. 5:9, "And they sang a new song, saying, 'You are worthy to take the book, and to open the seals thereof: for you were slain, and have redeemed us to God by your blood, out of every kindred and tongue, and people and nation.'" He redeemed us not with silver and gold, but with his own precious blood, by way of price, 1 Pet. 1:18,19. with his out-stretched and glorious arm, by way of power, Col. 1:13. he redeemed us freely, Eph. 1:7, fully Rom. 8:1, at the right time, Gal. 4:4, and out of special and particular love, John 17:9. In a word, he has redeemed us for ever, never more to come into bondage, 1 Pet. 1:5. John 10:28. O how lovely is Jesus Christ in the relation of a Redeemer to God's elect!

Secondly, *He is a lovely bridegroom* to all that he betroths to himself. How does the church glory in him, in the words following my text; "this is my Beloved, and this is my Friend, O ye daughters of Jerusalem!" Heaven and earth cannot show anyone like him, which needs no fuller proof than the following particulars:

1. That he betroths to himself, in mercy and in loving kindness, such deformed, defiled, and altogether unworthy souls as we are. We have no beauty, no goodness to make us desirable in his eyes; all the origins of his love to us are in his own breast, Deut. 7:7. He

chooses us, not because we were, but in order that he might make us lovely Eph. 5:27. He came to us when we lay in our blood, and said unto us, "Live"; and that was the time of love, Ezek. 16:6.

2. He expects no restitution from us, and yet gives himself, and all that he has, to us. Our poverty cannot enrich him, but he made himself poor to enrich us, 2 Cor. 8:9. 1 Cor. 3:22.

3. No husband loves the wife of his bosom, as much as Christ loved his people, Eph. 5:25. He loved the church and gave himself for it.

4. No one bears with weaknesses and provocations as Christ does; the church is called "the Lamb's wife," Rev. 21:9.

5. No husband is so undying and everlasting a husband as Christ is; death separates all other relations, but the soul's union with Christ is not dissolved in the grave. Indeed, the day of a believer's death is his marriage day, the day of his fullest enjoyment of Christ. No husband can say to his wife, what Christ says to the believer, "I will never leave you, nor forsake you," Heb. 13:5.

6. No bridegroom enriches his bride with such honours by marriage, as Christ does; he makes them related to God as their father, and from that day the mighty and glorious angels think it no dishonour to be their servants, Heb. 1:14. The angels will admire the beauty and glory of the spouse of Christ, Rev. 21:9.

7. No marriage was ever consummated with such triumphal proceedings as the marriage of Christ and believers shall be in heaven, Psalm 45:14,15. "She shall be brought to the king in raiment of needle-work, the virgins, her companions that follow her, shall be brought unto thee; with gladness and rejoicing shall they be brought; they shall enter into the king's palace." Among the Jews, the

Christ Altogether Lovely
John Flavel

marriage-house was called the house of praise; there was joy upon all hands, but nothing like the joy that will be in heaven when believers, the spouse of Christ, shall be brought there. God the Father will rejoice to behold the blessed accomplishment and confirmation of those glorious plans of his love. Jesus Christ, the Bridegroom will rejoice to see the travail of his soul, the blessed birth and product of all his bitter pains and agonies, Isa. 53:11. The Holy Spirit will rejoice to see the completion and perfection of that sanctifying design which was committed to his hand, 2 Cor. 5:5, to see those souls whom he once found as rough stones, now to shine as the bright, polished stones of the spiritual temple. Angels will rejoice: great was the joy when the foundation of this design was laid, in the incarnation of Christ, Luke 2:13. Great therefore must their joy be, when the top-stone is set up with shouting, crying, "Grace, grace." The saints themselves shall rejoice unspeakably, when they shall enter into the King's palace, and be forever with the Lord, 1 Thes. 4:17. Indeed there will be joy on all hands, except among the devils and damned, who shall gnash their teeth with envy at the everlasting advancement and glory of believers. Thus Christ is altogether lovely, in the relation of a Bridegroom.

Thirdly, *Christ is altogether lovely, in the relation of an Advocate*. 1 John 2:1, "If any man sin, we have an advocate with the Father, Jesus Christ the righteous, and he is the Propitiation." It is he that pleads the cause of believers in heaven. He appears for them in the presence of God, to prevent any new alienation, and to continue the state of friendship and peace between God and us. In this relation Christ is altogether lovely. For,

1. He makes our cause his own, and acts for us in heaven, as if for himself, Heb. 4:15. He is touched with a most tender

understanding of our troubles and dangers, and is not only one with us by way of representation, but also one with us in respect of sympathy and affection.

2. Christ our Advocate tracks our cause and business in heaven, as his great and primary design and business. For this reason in Hebrews 7:25. he is said to "live for ever to make intercession for us." It is as if our concerns were so attended to by him there, that all the glory and honour which is paid him in heaven would not divert him one moment from our business.

3. He pleads the cause of believers by his blood. Unlike other advocates, it is not enough for him to lay out only words, which is a cheaper way of pleading; but he pleads for us by the voice of his own blood, as in Heb. 12:24, where we are said to be come "to the blood of sprinkling, that speaketh better things than that of Abel." Every wound he received for us on earth is a mouth opened to plead with God on our behalf in heaven. And hence it is, that in Rev. 5:6 he is represented standing before God, as a lamb that had been slain; as it were exhibiting and revealing in heaven those deadly wounds received on earth from the justice of God, on our account. Other advocates spend their breath, Christ spends his blood.

4. He pleads the cause of believers freely. Other advocates plead for reward, and empty the purses, while they plead the causes of their clients.

5. In a word, he obtains for us all the mercies for which he pleads. No cause miscarries in his hand, which he undertakes, Rom. 8:33, 34. what a lovely Advocate is Christ for believers!

Fourthly, *Christ is altogether lovely in the relation of a friend,* for in this relation he is pleased to acknowledge his people, Luke

Christ Altogether Lovely
John Flavel

12:4, 5. There are certain things in which one friend manifests his affection and friendship to another, but there is not one like Christ. For,

1. No friend is so open-hearted to his friend as Christ is to his people: he reveals the very counsels and secrets of his heart to them. John 15:15. "Henceforth I call you not servants, for the servant knows not what his Lord does; but I have called you friends; for all things that I have heard of my Father, I have made known unto you.

2. No friend in the world is so generous and bountiful to his friend, as Jesus Christ is to believers; he parts with his very blood for them; "Greater love (he says) has no man than this, that a man lay down his life for his friends," John 15:13. He has exhausted the precious treasures of his invaluable blood to pay our debts. O what a lovely friend is Jesus Christ to believers!

3. No friend sympathizes so tenderly with his friend in affliction, as Jesus Christ does with his friends: "In all our afflictions he is afflicted," Heb. 4:15. He feels all our sorrows, needs and burdens as his own. This is why it is said that the sufferings of believers are called the sufferings of Christ, Col. 1:24.

4. No friend in the world takes that contentment in his friends, as Jesus Christ does in believers. Song of Songs 4:9. "You have ravished my heart, (he says to the spouse) you have ravished my heart with one of your eyes, with one chain of your neck." The Hebrew, here rendered "ravished," signifies to puff up, or to make one proud: how the Lord Jesus is pleased to glory in his people! How he is taken and delighted with those gracious ornaments which himself bestows upon them! There is no friend so lovely as Christ.

5. No friend in the world loves his friend with as impassioned and strong affection as Jesus Christ loves believers. Jacob loved

Rachel, and endured for her sake the parching heat of summer and cold of winter; but Christ endured the storms of the wrath of God, the heat of his indignation, for our sakes. David manifested his love to Absalom, in wishing, "O that I had died for you!" Christ manifested his love to us, not in wishes that he had died, but in death itself, in our stead, and for our sakes.

6. No friend in the world is so constant and unchangeable in friendship as Christ is. John 13:1, "Having loved his own which were in the world, he loved them unto the end." He bears with millions of provocations and wrongs, and yet will not break friendship with his people. Peter denied him, yet he will not disown him; but after his resurrection he says, "Go, tell the disciples, and tell Peter." Let him not think he has forfeited by that sin of his, his interest in me. Though he denied me, I will not disown him, Mark 16:7. how lovely is Christ in the relation of a friend!

I might further show you the loveliness of Christ in his ordinances and in his providences, in his communion with us and communications to us, but there is no end of the account of Christ's loveliness: I will rather choose to press believers to their duties towards this altogether lovely Christ, which I shall briefly conclude in a few words.

Christ Altogether Lovely
John Flavel

APPLICATION

1. *Is Jesus Christ altogether lovely?* Then I beseech you set your souls upon this lovely Jesus. I am sure such an object as has been here represented, would compel love from the coldest breast and hardest heart. Away with those empty nothings, away with this vain deceitful world, which deserves not the thousandth part of the love you give it. Let all stand aside and give way to Christ. O if only you knew his worth and excellency, what he is in himself, what he has done for you, and deserved from you, you would need no arguments of mine to persuade you to love him!

2. *Esteem nothing lovely except as it is enjoyed in Christ, or used for the sake of Christ.* Love nothing for itself, love nothing separate from Jesus Christ. In two things we all sin in love of created things. We sin in the excess of our affections, loving them above the proper value of mere created things. We also sin in the inordinacy of our affections, that is to say we give our love for created things a priority it should never have.

3. *Let us all be humbled for the corruption of our hearts* that are so eager in their affections for vanities and trifles and so hard to be persuaded to the love of Christ, who is altogether lovely. O how many pour out streams of love and delight upon the vain and empty created thing; while no arguments can draw forth one drop of love from their stubborn and unbelieving hearts to Jesus Christ! I have read of one Joannes Mollius, who was observed to go often alone, and weep bitterly; and being pressed by a friend to know the cause

of his troubles, said "O! it grieves me that I cannot bring this heart of mine to love Jesus Christ more fervently."

4. *Represent Christ to the world as he is, by your behaviour towards him.* Is he altogether lovely? Let all the world see and know that he is so, by your delights in him and communion with him; zeal for him, and readiness to part with any other lovely thing upon his account. Proclaim his excellencies to the world, as the spouse did in these verses. Persuade them how much your beloved is better than any other beloved. Show his glorious excellencies as you speak of him; hold him forth to others, as he is in himself: altogether lovely. See that you "walk worthy of him unto all well pleasing," Col. 1:10. "Show forth the praises of Christ," 1 Pet. 2:19. Let not that "worthy name be blasphemed through you," James 2:7. He is glorious in himself, and he is sure to put glory upon you; take heed that you do not put shame and dishonours upon him; he has committed his honour to you, do not betray that trust.

Never be ashamed to be counted as a Christian: he is altogether lovely; he can never be a shame to you; it will be your great sin to be ashamed of him. Some men glory in their shame; do not let yourself be ashamed of your glory. If you will be ashamed of Christ now, he will be ashamed of you when he shall appear in his own glory, and the glory of all his holy angels. Be ashamed of nothing but sin; and among other sins, be ashamed especially for this sin, that you have no more love for him who is altogether lovely.

6. *Be willing to leave every thing that is lovely upon earth*, in order that you may be with the altogether lovely Lord Jesus Christ in heaven. Lift up your voices with the bride, Rev. 20:20 "Come Lord Jesus, come quickly." It is true, you must pass through the pangs of

death into his intimacy and enjoyment; but surely it is worth suffering much more than that to be with this lovely Jesus. "The Lord direct your hearts into the love of God, and the patient waiting for Jesus Christ," 2 Thes. 3:5.

7. *Let the loveliness of Christ draw all men to him.* Is loveliness in the creature so attractive? And can the transcendent loveliness of Christ draw none? O the blindness of man! If you see no beauty in Christ that causes you to desire him, it is because the god of this world has blinded your minds.

8. *Strive to be Christ-like, if ever you would be lovely in the eyes of God and man.* Certainly, my brethren, it is only the Spirit of Christ within you, and the beauty of Christ upon you, which can make you lovely persons. The more you resemble him in holiness, the more will you show of true excellence and loveliness; and the more frequent and spiritual your communication and communion with Christ is, the more of the beauty and loveliness of Christ will be stamped upon your spirits, changing you into the same image, from glory to glory. Amen.

Christ Altogether Lovely
John Flavel

Christ Altogether Lovely
John Flavel

Index of Scripture References

Deuteronomy
7:7

Job
4:21

Psalms
45:2   45:2   45:14-15   73:26

Proverbs
8:11

Song of Solomon
4:9   5:8   5:16

Isaiah
49:6   53:11   61:1

Ezekiel
16:6

Malachi
4:2

Mark
16:7

Luke
1:78   2:13   12:4-5

John
1:14   3:34   10:28   13:1   15:13   15:15   17:9

Acts
17:27

Romans
8:1   8:33-34

Christ Altogether Lovely
John Flavel

1 Corinthians
1:30   3:22

2 Corinthians
5:5   8:9

Galatians
4:4

Ephesians
1:7   5:25   5:27

Colossians
1:10   1:13   1:17   1:19   1:20   1:24

1 Thessalonians
1:10

2 Thessalonians
3:5

1 Timothy
3:16

Hebrews
1:14   4:15   4:15   7:25   7:25   12:24   13:5   13:8

James
2:7

1 Peter
1:5   1:18-19   2:19

1 John
2:1

Revelation
5:6   5:9   20:20   21:9   21:9

Christ Altogether Lovely
John Flavel

Christ Altogether Lovely
John Flavel

Christ Altogether Lovely
John Flavel

Pathways To The Past

Each volume stands alone as an Individual Book
Each volume stands together with others
to enhance the value of your collection

Build your Personal, Pastoral or Church Library
Pathways To The Past contains an ever-expanding list of
Christendom's most influential authors

Augustine of Hippo
Athanasius
E. M. Bounds
John Bunyan
Robert Lewis Darby
Brother Lawrence
Jessie Penn-Lewis
Bernard of Clairvaux
Andrew Murray
Watchman Nee
Arthur W. Pink
Thomas Watson
Hannah Whitall Smith
R. A. Torrey
A. W. Tozer
Jean-Pierre de Caussade
And many, many more.

Christ Altogether Lovely
John Flavel

Christ Altogether Lovely
John Flavel

Christ Altogether Lovely
John Flavel

www.ingramcontent.com/pod-product-compliance
Lightning Source LLC
Chambersburg PA
CBHW050336120526
44592CB00014B/2213